AEROSPACE ENGINEERING
AND THE Principles of Flight

ENGINEERING IN ACTION

Crabtree Publishing Company

www.crabtreebooks.com

Anne Rooney

Crabtree Publishing Company
www.crabtreebooks.com

This book is dedicated to the memory of a brilliant young aerospace engineer, Alexander Ward (1989-2012)

Author: Anne Rooney
Publishing plan research and development:
Sean Charlebois, Reagan Miller
Crabtree Publishing Company
Photo research: James Nixon
Editors: Paul Humphrey, Adrianna Morganelli, James Nixon
Proofreader: Kathy Middleton
Layout design: sprout.uk.com
Cover design and logo: Margaret Amy Salter
Production coordinator and prepress technician: Margaret Amy Salter
Print coordinator: Katherine Berti

Produced for Crabtree Publishing Company
by Discovery Books

Photographs:
Alamy: pp. 4 (Denis Hallinan), 11 top (Greg Meland), 12 (The Print Collector), 21 top (Images Etc Ltd), 24 left (Thierry GRUN—Aero).
Corbis: pp. 16 (Carla Cioffi/NASA), 17 (Imagechina), 22 (Larry Downing/REUTERS), 28 (Gene Blevins/Los Angeles Daily News).
NASA: pp. 20, 21 bottom, 23 top (Sean Smith), 23 bottom (JPL), 29 top and bottom.
Shutterstock: pp. 5 (Ilja Masik), 6 (Carlos Caetano), 9 top (David Acosta Allely), 15 top (Brian K.), 19 (Jordan Tan), 26 top (Niels Quist), 27 bottom (Rtimages).
Thinkstock: cover
Wikimedia: pp. 7 (Library of Congress), 11 bottom (Nigel Coates), 15 middle (Great Images in NASA), 15 bottom (Library of Congress), 18 (Library of Congress), 24 right (Guy Pasquerella), 25 (Ssgt Aaron D. Allmon II/USAF).

Library and Archives Canada Cataloguing in Publication

Rooney, Anne
    Aerospace engineering and the principles of flight / Anne Rooney.

(Engineering in action)
Includes index.
Issued also in electronic formats.
ISBN 978-0-7787-7495-2 (bound).--ISBN 978-0-7787-7500-3 (pbk.)

    1. Aerospace engineering--Juvenile literature. 2. Flight--Juvenile literature. I. Title. II. Series: Engineering in action (St. Catharines, Ont.)

TL547.R655 2012   j629.1   C2012-906841-1

Library of Congress Cataloging-in-Publication Data

CIP available at Library of Congress

Crabtree Publishing Company
www.crabtreebooks.com   1-800-387-7650

Printed in Hong Kong/012013/BK20121102

Published in Canada
Crabtree Publishing
616 Welland Ave.
St. Catharines, ON
L2M 5V6

Published in the United States
Crabtree Publishing
PMB 59051
350 Fifth Avenue, 59th Floor
New York, New York 10118

Published in the United Kingdom
Crabtree Publishing
Maritime House
Basin Road North, Hove
BN41 1WR

Published in Australia
Crabtree Publishing
3 Charles Street
Coburg North
VIC, 3058

CONTENTS

WHAT IS AEROSPACE ENGINEERING?

Flying has fascinated humans for centuries. Now flight is an everyday experience. This is thanks to aerospace engineers who design and improve planes, helicopters, and even spacecraft.

Aerospace engineers

Aerospace engineers work on the construction of aircraft (aeronautics) and spacecraft (astronautical engineering). They deal with the issues relating to flight, including the forces that act on an aircraft, such as gravity. Aerospace engineers often work closely with scientists and people in other branches of engineering, such as electrical and mechanical engineering.

In aerospace engineering, people work together on a project. They bring different ideas and knowledge to find the best solution to a problem.

It's not rocket science: Engineering and science are closely linked, but they are not the same. Engineers design, test, and build rockets and planes. Scientists explore, discover, and explain the ways that rockets and planes work. Often, scientists work to investigate problems that engineers come across. The results of their work help engineers to make progress. The work of engineers sometimes leads to new areas of scientific investigation.

The design for a new plane often begins on a computer screen.

4

The design process: The earliest pioneers of flight launched themselves bravely into the air in craft of their own design, sometimes with disastrous results. The modern aerospace industry follows a well-established process to make sure designs for craft are the best and safest they can be before anyone takes a risk flying them. They follow an eight-step process to design, build, and test new designs.

1. Start with a problem or task that has to be done

↓

2. Work out the requirements of the task

↓

3. Brainstorm ways of tackling the problem or task

↓

4. Choose the best possible method

↓

5. Make a model of the new item

↓

6. Test the model to see how well it works

7. Improve the design if testing shows any problems

↓

8. Get people working on the new design

THE FIRST AEROSPACE ENGINEER?

Archytas lived in ancient Greece 2,400 years ago (428–350 BCE). He experimented with kites and model flying machines, including a wooden bird called the Pigeon. The Pigeon was propelled by the movement of air in or through it. Its longest flight was over 650 feet (200 m).

HOW FLIGHT WORKS

Anything that flies must move through the air, just as any ship must move through water. Aeronautical engineers need a good understanding of how air affects flying craft.

A hot-air balloon rises because the heated air is less dense than the cold air outside the balloon.

Properties of air: Air is invisible, but it has many properties that must be taken into account. Air has **mass**, and moves. Its **density** changes with temperature. Aerospace engineers need to understand how the mass, movement, pressure, and temperature of air affect a plane or other craft. They work with the forces produced by the air to design craft that work safely and effectively.

Light and heavy craft

Hot-air balloons and airships are lighter than air, but aircraft such as planes and helicopters are heavier than air.

When air is heated, the **molecules** of gas move around more, requiring more space. The air in a hot-air balloon (called the "envelope") has a lower density, which means it also has a lower mass than the same volume of cold air outside. The lower density of hot air inside makes the balloon rise.

	Normal Air	Air in a hot-air balloon
Temperature	68 °F (20 °C)	210 °F (99 °C)
Density	1.2027 oz/ft³ (1.2041 kg/m³)	0.8968 oz/ft³ (0.8978 kg/m³)
Mass of 2,500 cubic meters	6,636.47 lb (3,010.25 kg)	4,948.28 lb (2,244.5 kg)

Since a hot-air balloon is much lighter than air, it can easily lift a basket containing the crew and a burner to produce the hot air.

Airships are filled with helium, a gas that is lighter than air. They also rely on low density to make them rise.

All planes, helicopters, and spacecraft are heavier than air. Complex calculations involving different forces are needed to get them off the ground, keep them in the air, and control them safely.

This illustration shows the Montgolfier brothers' balloon flying over the Seine River in Paris.

THE FIRST BALLOON FLIGHT

The first flight in a balloon not secured to the ground with ropes was in Paris in 1783. The balloon was constructed by the Montgolfier brothers, Joseph and Étienne. Joseph was interested in why sparks rise from a fire. He made a small balloon from thin cloth and lit a fire under it, making it rise into the air. He then experimented with larger balloons. In 1783, he lifted a sheep, a duck, and a rooster together into the air in a hot-air balloon. The first manned balloon was set to be piloted by prisoners sentenced to death, but science teacher Jean-François Pilâtre de Rozier and François Laurentd'Arlandes, volunteered instead. They flew 5.5 miles (nine km) in 25 minutes and landed safely.

PILÂTRE DE ROZIER

FORCES IN ACTION

There are four forces that work on aircraft: lift, drag, weight, and thrust. Aerospace engineers use and balance these forces to make aircraft take off, move forward, and land.

Lift and weight:

Lift acts at right angles to the direction of the flow of the air. While a plane moves forward horizontally, lift pushes the plane vertically upward. When a plane climbs at an angle, lift operates at an angle, too. Lift is produced by the pressure of moving air pushed out of the way by the wings of an aircraft.

Weight operates downward, toward Earth. It is produced by the force of **gravity** pulling on an object. While the mass of an object stays the same throughout the universe, weight varies with gravity. Gravity on the moon is about one-sixth of gravity on Earth. An object would weigh only 16 percent of its weight on Earth.

An aircraft has to counteract the pull of gravity (weight) in order to launch and stay airborne. Weight and lift operate in opposite directions when a plane is flying horizontally.

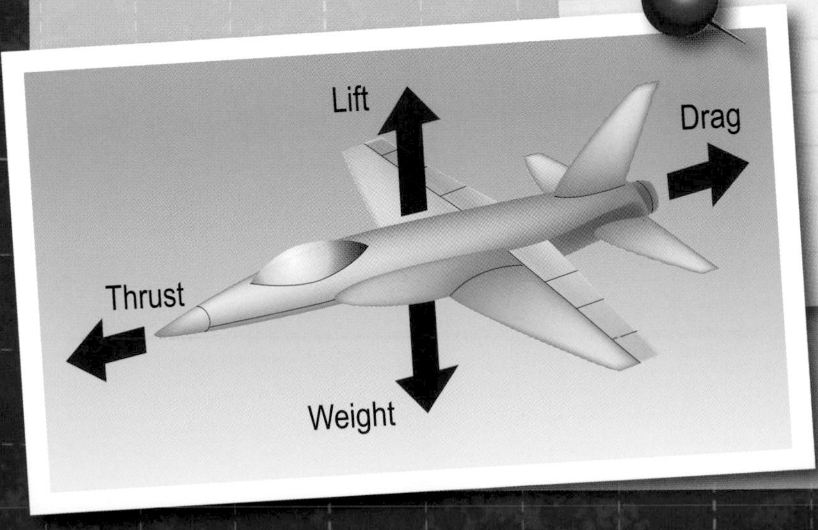

The four forces of lift, drag, weight, and thrust operate at right angles to each other when a plane flies horizontally.

Drag and thrust: Drag is the force that slows down an object moving through a liquid or gas. Drag increases with velocity (speed). You can experience drag yourself if you try to walk through deep water. The faster you try to move, the harder it becomes.

For a plane to move against the force of drag, it needs thrust. This is the forward movement provided by the engine in powered flight.

A helicopter's lift is produced by the **rotor** spinning against the air.

Fuel and flight

To provide thrust, a plane needs to carry fuel. This adds to the weight, and so the plane needs more lift. Engineers work with scientists to develop the best materials to make planes light but strong. Structural engineers advise on how to make the strongest structures using the least material. Chemists develop fuels that provide the energy needed, yet will stay in liquid form at the low temperature and pressure of high **altitudes**.

The pressure of a fluid decreases and its speed of flow increases as it moves through a narrower space.

BERNOULLI AND FLUID DYNAMICS

Water and air are both fluids—they flow over and around surfaces. The way fluids move is described by fluid dynamics. In 1738, the Dutch mathematician Daniel Bernoulli showed in a study that the pressure of a moving fluid in a **venturi tube** decreases as its speed increases. This discovery was very important in aerospace design because it showed that the fast-flowing air going over an airplane wing is at lower pressure than the air moving more slowly beneath the wing. This difference in pressure can create lift to make aircraft go upward.

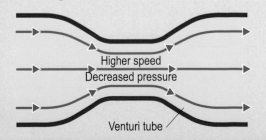

Higher speed
Decreased pressure

Venturi tube

BALANCING FORCES

For a plane to fly at a constant speed and height, the four forces must be balanced so that weight and lift are equal, and drag and thrust are equal. When a plane ascends (goes up) or descends (goes down) these pairs of forces are not equal.

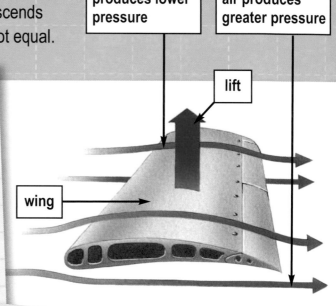

faster-moving air produces lower pressure

slower-moving air produces greater pressure

lift

wing

Balancing lift and weight:

To counteract the weight of an aircraft pulling it toward Earth, aerospace engineers need to maximize lift. Aircraft wings are designed so that air flows over the top of the wing quickly, making an area of low pressure. This shape is called an airfoil. The air pressure below the wing is greater, and this helps to push the wing upward, increasing lift.

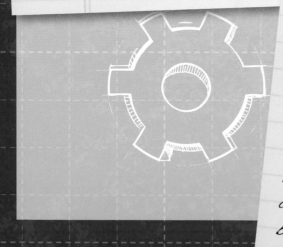

Balancing thrust and drag:

When thrust and drag are equal, a plane moves at a steady speed. To accelerate, or move faster, the plane needs more thrust. The plane then goes faster until the increasing drag is again equal to the thrust, and the speed stabilizes.

Reducing thrust slows the plane down. As the plane slows, or decelerates, the drag reduces. When the two forces are equal again, the plane goes at a steady, but slower speed.

The force of air at high pressure beneath a plane moving quickly, pushes it upward off the runway.

Up and down

A plane rises when lift is greater than weight, and descends when weight is greater than lift. But how do you change the lift of a plane parked on a runway?

As a plane accelerates along the runway, air above the plane is at lower pressure than air below the plane, producing lift that eventually raises the plane off the ground. You can test this yourself by pushing a toy boat through water. As you push faster, the front of the boat starts to lift upward.

GEORGE CAYLEY, 1773-1857

This replica of Cayley's glider is at the Yorkshire Air Museum in England.

George Cayley was the first modern aeronautical engineer. He set out the idea of an airplane with unmoving wings that had different engineering systems to work with lift, **propulsion**, and control. He was also the first to identify the four forces of lift, drag, weight, and thrust. In 1849, Cayley designed the first successful glider—a plane with no engine—to carry a human. He also designed the cambered **airfoil**, which is an airfoil with unequal top and bottom curves that help give more lift than a **symmetrical** airfoil.

ACTIVITY

In this activity, you will look at how the properties of air can be used to help things to fly. You will need two identical plastic bags, two identical action figures, string, and scissors. You will also need a stopwatch, or a stopwatch feature on your cell phone.

No parachute!
Stand somewhere you can drop your action figure safely. You can use a stairwell if you are sure no one is underneath, or you can stand safely on a chair or table. Drop the action figure.

Try to time the fall with the stopwatch. It is probably too fast for you to do so.

Making the parachute: Take one of the plastic bags and cut out a square of plastic with sides of 12 inches (30 cm). Cut the corners off the square to make an octagon.

Cut a hole in each corner. You can use a hole punch if you find it easier.

Cut eight pieces of string 16 inches (40 cm) long. Thread one through each hole and tie it in place. Hold the middle of the parachute with one hand so that the strings hang down, then tie them together. Tie the action figure to the strings.

Parachutes are not just for fun. Aerospace engineers design parachutes for emergency use by pilots and for spacecraft landing back on Earth.

Now drop the action figure from the same height and time how long it takes to fall to the floor. Repeat this three times, recording the times in a table.

Make a second parachute, from a square with sides of 24 inches (60 cm) and repeat the trials. After you have recorded the times find the average time for each parachute size by adding the three times together, then dividing by three.

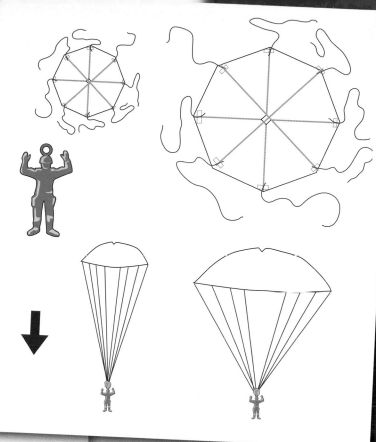

Make your parachutes identical in all aspects except the size.

Parachute	Time 1	Time 2	Time 3	Average
None	-	-	-	-
12 inches (30 cm)				
24 inches (60 cm)				

How does the size of a parachute affect the speed of descent?

Make a small hole in the middle of one of the parachutes and drop it again.

What difference does the hole make?

How do you think forces are acting on the parachute?

TAKING FLIGHT

Humans first took inspiration from birds in their quest for flight, but modern jets and rockets owe very little to natural models of flight. Instead, they work by forcing gases out of the back at high pressure—just like blowing up a balloon and releasing it makes the balloon rush away from you.

Unpowered flight

After hot-air balloons, the next experiments in flight were with large kites and gliders. The German aviator Otto Lilienthal (1848-1896) made detailed studies of how birds fly and then built a series of gliders. His experiments began unsuccessfully with wings strapped onto his body. Eventually he discovered how to use lift from the wind and swing his body weight to control his gliders.

The Wright brothers

The era of controlled, powered flight began with Orville and Wilbur Wright's *Flyer* at Kill Devil Hills, North Carolina, U.S.A., in 1903. The Wright brothers made a plane that used a small gasoline-powered engine of their own design. From their tests, they found that the flow of air around an aircraft can make it unstable and wobble in three directions: tipping up and down from front to back—(roll); wobbling from left to right—(pitch); spinning around—(yaw).

Propulsion: Propulsion, or thrust, is provided by an engine burning fuel, such as gasoline. There are two main types of engine: shaft engines and reaction engines.

A shaft engine drives a propeller or rotor. The earliest planes, including the Wright's Flyer, all used shaft engines.

A reaction engine uses the pressure of exhaust (waste gas from burning fuel) forced out at the rear to push the craft forward. Jet and rocket engines are types of reaction engine. The first turbojet engines were used in World War II planes. Rocket propulsion is most efficient at very high speeds and is better suited to spacecraft than aircraft.

Controlling pitch, roll, and yaw: The Wrights tried to control roll using wing warping— a system of cables and pulleys that let them twist the trailing edges of the wings. During the early 1900s, many aviators experimented with flaps called **ailerons** to control roll, and these are still used today.

A **rudder** works in the same way to control yaw and is fixed to the vertical tail fin. **Elevators** are flaps, similar to the rudder, on the horizontal tailplane that control pitch.

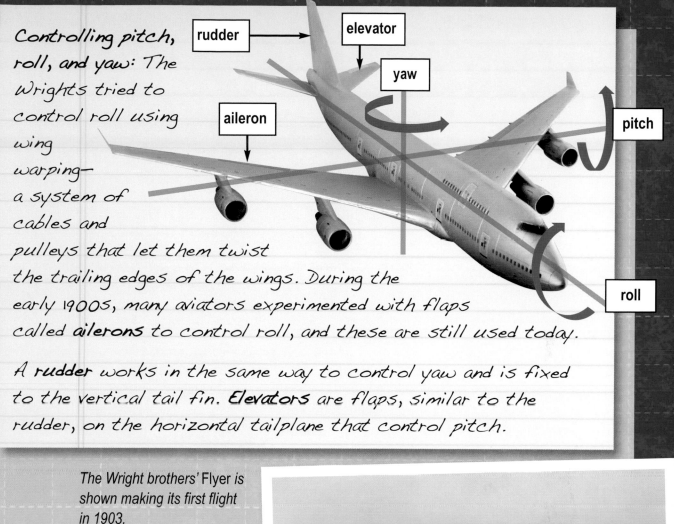

The Wright brothers' Flyer is shown making its first flight in 1903.

The Wright brothers are shown conducting their experiment with wing warping using an unmanned glider.

WORKING IN AEROSPACE

There are many career opportunities in aerospace engineering. Engineers work on whole craft or parts of them, such as engines or systems that guide them.

Areas of work

Aerospace engineers are involved at all stages of the design, development, construction, and maintenance of aircraft, spacecraft, and missiles. Skilled engineers can move on to senior roles managing and overseeing the work of teams to design, build, and manufacture craft.

Designers

Engineers work with a team of experts in different areas of aerospace engineering to design new craft or components. This can involve working on materials and fuels; creating streamlined, **aerodynamic** designs; or planning guidance systems—the computer systems used to control and navigate craft. Considerations such as passenger comfort, cost reduction, and protection of the environment are also important in the design of craft.

When a rocket takes off, it is the end of years of work by aerospace engineers.

Mechanics

Aerospace mechanics are involved in putting together models, **prototypes**, and final designs. This is a hands-on job, working with aircraft components and requiring some physical strength. Mechanics might specialize in particular areas, such as landing gear, airframe (body of the craft), engines, or electrical systems. Mechanics also maintain craft to keep them flying safely. Maintenance includes checking and repairing components and systems, and sometimes investigating a fault to find its cause and fix it.

*Test engineer: Testing happens at different stages of development. Computer modeling to investigate how a planned craft will behave requires advanced computer programming. Other engineers work with physical models, parts, or whole craft. They test them in **wind tunnels**, laboratories, or in flight to make sure they work and to find out how far they can be pushed before they break.*

Forensic engineer: Forensic engineers investigate crashes and failures. They work from recovered debris and the black box— a device that records what happens in a plane in flight—to discover the cause of a crash. If a design fault or broken component causes a crash, the design of the craft will be changed to prevent the same thing from happening again.

SKILLS NEEDED

To work in aerospace engineering you will need a good knowledge of engineering and physics, and computer and mathematical skills. Engineers must work cooperatively and share ideas, so good teamwork and communication skills are essential. You will also need to be able to think logically and take a creative approach to solving problems.

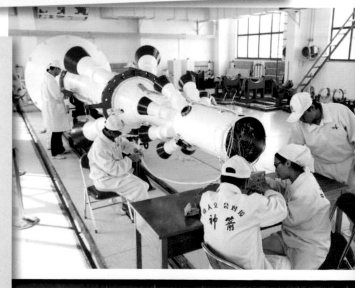

STARTING THE DESIGN PROCESS

All new projects start with a problem or proposal. For example, perhaps there is a need for a new craft or component, or an improvement to an existing design.

Most early planes were biplanes—they had two pairs of wings arranged one above the other. The box structure added strength to wings made of light, flimsy materials.

Identifying the problem: The need for a design solution can come from many sources. Sometimes there is an entirely new project—a military force wants to commission a new fleet of fighter jets, or an airline wants a new line of passenger planes, or a space agency wants a shuttlecraft. The design problem will set out a description of what is wanted, what the craft needs to do, and what it should be like.

EARLY WINGS: BIPLANE AND MONOPLANE

The earliest aviators struggled with the need to make plane wings light but strong. They had to be light to get off the ground, but they also had to be strong enough to support the craft and pilot. These two requirements made many materials unsuitable—either they were not strong enough or they were not light enough. Most planes were made of fabric stretched over a wooden frame. This is very light, but not strong. Trial and error showed that a biplane design, with pairs of wings arranged vertically and struts between them, provided structural strength using flimsy materials. It also allowed smaller wings to bear a heavier load. When strong and light aluminum alloy wings became common in the 1920s, monoplanes, or aircraft with only one pair of wings, took over.

A DESIGN WITH CONSTRAINTS

The Boeing 787 Dreamliner is a new, very large passenger aircraft. The plane is built by Boeing for sale to commercial airlines, so its design had to meet the demands of more than one customer. Customers also required that the plane should be environmentally friendly. As a result, it produces fewer harmful gases than other planes, it is made of materials that can be recycled when the plane is too old to fly, and fewer hazardous materials are used in its manufacture.

Criteria and constraints: Criteria are requirements the design must meet. For example, if the project is to design a plane to carry 600 passengers on long-distance flights, the airline might specify that there must be a business class area with good standards of comfort.

Constraints are limits to the design. They might include the amount of money that can be spent, the materials available, or international regulations. Some constraints can't be changed by engineers. For instance, the strength of a particular metal can't be changed. Other constraints, such as how much money is available, are set by the customer.

WORKING WITH IDEAS

In the past, many aviators worked alone or with a very small team. In a modern setting, though, engineers work together to come up with possible solutions to a problem, develop ideas, and explore possibilities.

Brainstorming: When a new design or solution is needed, a team of engineers often begins by brainstorming the problem. A lot of expert staff, often with different skills, get together to come up with ideas relating to any aspect of the problem. Everyone is encouraged to contribute, even making odd suggestions that might seem strange or unusual. There is no criticism of ideas at this point. In fact, it is often ideas that at first seem unpromising that lead to original solutions and great steps forward.

Choosing the best solution: After brainstorming, the ideas are evaluated. The team decides which ideas best meet the needs and constraints of the project and chooses one or more of the ideas to develop further. This step is often repeated several times, as ideas are worked on and then rejected if they are not working.

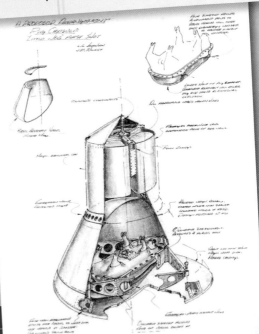

A pen and ink sketch is a good way of developing a new idea. This design from 1959 is for a capsule to carry a pig into space!

Brainstorming and crazy ideas

In the 1950s, engineers at NASA were designing spacecraft to take humans into space. One problem was getting a capsule back to Earth safely. Engineers began with streamlined designs that would reduce drag, but in all cases the capsule would overheat and put the astronauts in danger. They brainstormed ideas, believing the problem that had to be solved was how to keep the craft cool. But engineer Max Faget had a different idea—what if the problem wasn't how to cool off the craft, but rather how to keep the heat away from it in the first place? After lunch one day, he sketched a new design on his napkin that showed a blunt-shaped capsule. It would be carried into space on top of a rocket. Faget dropped paper plates out of the window to test the aerodynamic properties of shapes. His

*A meteor entering Earth's atmosphere creates heat by **compressing** the air in its path and burns up.*

shape was not aerodynamic at all—it was so badly streamlined that it would create a massive shockwave around the craft, keeping the heat away from it.

Although the idea seemed crazy at first, the team decided to test it. Wind-tunnel tests showed the "gumdrop" design to be the most successful at reducing heat. It was adopted and has been adapted over time, but is still in use today.

In 1965, the Gemini VII spacecraft used the gumdrop shape developed by Max Faget.

PROTOTYPES

Once aerospace engineers have designed a solution, they will build prototypes to test the design.

A model of an airplane is prepared for testing.

Making models and prototypes: First, the new craft, system, or part is modeled using computer software. Engineers use this to test how the system will behave in different circumstances—in different weather conditions, for instance, or to see what happens if a part breaks or fails. They can also use it to investigate the performance of different materials.

Next, engineers make physical models and prototypes. Not all of these are fully functional or full size. The aerodynamics of the aircraft's shape can be tested on an empty shell or a scaled model, for instance.

Safety first

Aircraft and spacecraft are safety-critical systems. This means if they go wrong, lives are in danger. It is important to make sure all the parts work as planned. They must be fail-safe systems—if something goes wrong, it should fail in a way that keeps people safe.

A huge wind tunnel is used to test a full-size plane.

Testing: Prototypes are tested in different ways. Aerodynamic shapes are tested in a wind tunnel. This is a closed tube with a powerful fan system used to create different wind conditions and speeds. Even the early aviator Orville Wright used a simple wind tunnel to test his designs.

Wind tunnels use smoke, bubbles of liquid, or threads to help show the flow of the air. Engineers sometimes use special pressure-sensitive paint on the model. The paint glows more or less brightly according to the pressure on the surface.

The final prototype of an airplane is flown by a test pilot. Each test pilot specializes in one type of plane, such as airliners or fighter planes. The pilot's judgment is important, but computers also monitor the craft's performance.

This lander made its first explorations of Mars in 2012 but was tested on Earth before the mission.

TESTING SPACECRAFT

Engineers working on spacecraft test them on Earth in conditions that reproduce those that the craft will encounter in space. They use hostile environments, such as the deep sea or scorching deserts, to provide great pressure or heat. Equipment that will be used in space is tested in anti-gravity chambers that match the weightlessness experienced in space.

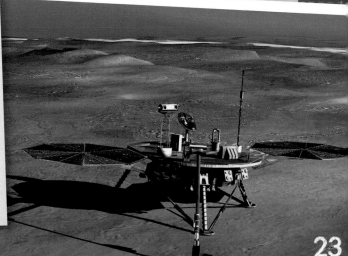

BETTER AND BETTER

Often, testing reveals problems with a prototype. These feed back into the design process, and the cycle is repeated. When at last a successful design emerges, it goes into production.

Improving the design: Results from testing are evaluated by the engineering team. If there is room for improvement, or if any faults are revealed, the design is modified to improve it. The new design must be modeled and tested all over again—and the process might be repeated many times.

In 1937, the giant airship the Hindenburg caught fire in New Jersey, killing 35 people.

AIRSHIPS FOR THE FUTURE

Airships are giant balloons, usually sausage-shaped, filled with helium and with an engine and guidance system to steer them. The earliest airships were filled with hydrogen, but hydrogen is a very flammable gas. After some disastrous accidents, airships were built to use helium instead. The buoyancy (ability to float) of an airship is changed to make it go up or down. Airships used to do this by collecting water or dumping gas to change the weight of the craft. The latest designs of airship (left) try to make the system more controllable. They use a compressor to change the pressure of the helium. Some new airships have solar panels, too, to reduce their need for fuel. This is useful for unmanned airships being used to monitor the weather. These airships need to stay in the air for weeks at a time.

Repeating the cycle: failure and success

A stealth aircraft is a military plane designed to fly over enemy territory without being spotted. The first American stealth plane was the Lockheed U2, developed in 1952. At first, engineers believed by flying high, a plane would avoid enemy **radar**, but this proved to be wrong. Next, they brainstormed ways of confusing radar. Two ideas were chosen, developed, and prototyped: covering the plane in a wire mesh coated with iron paint, or hanging wires from the nose and tail. Neither method worked well, and both reduced the plane's performance.

In 1975, engineers proposed an idea so unpromising it was called the *Hopeless Diamond*. By giving the plane a faceted surface (made up of lots of small flat surfaces rather than smooth curves), they hoped to hide it from radar. Years later and with many alterations, the *Hopeless Diamond* developed into the successful F-117 fighter plane!

The U.S. Air Force F-117A Nighthawk fighter plane was developed from the Hopeless Diamond *concept.*

Communicating the solution: Engineers need good communication skills. The final design must be presented in such a way that others can understand it and can use it to put the design into production.

New solutions to problems are also published in journals so that other aerospace engineers can benefit from and build on the work.

DESIGN CHALLENGE: MAKE A GLIDER

The best way to understand the process aerospace engineers go through is to try it yourself.

1: The problem: Your task is to build a glider that will fly smoothly.

2: Requirements and constraints: Decide how far you want the plane to fly and in what conditions. Will you use it indoors or outdoors? How will the requirements differ?

What are the constraints on your design? Think about the materials and tools you have available. For instance, you might use paper, plastic foam sheets, or balsa wood.

3: Brainstorm!: Research model glider designs on the web or in books. Make notes and sketches of models you might try.

4: Choose a solution: Evaluate the designs against the requirements and restrictions you identified. Choose the size and materials and think about the techniques and tools you will use. Are there any designs you must rule out because you don't have or can't afford the materials or tools?

Could you make a more complex glider if you worked with a partner?

Choose the solution that you think is most likely to work well.

5: Make a prototype: Your final prototype must be in full working order and made from the right materials. You don't need to include anything that won't affect performance, such as the final color.

6: Test the prototype: Test your prototype by launching it. Make repeated test flights, launching the model with the same amount of force each time and measuring how far it flies. Draw up a table of distances and find the average.

You could design your own wind tunnel to investigate the flow of air around your craft. Use a fan or hair dryer and a large tube, and stick thin thread to the body and wings so that they are carried in the air current.

7: Improve the design: Are there any problems with your glider? Figure out how to fix them.

Can you think of any adjustments or improvements you could make? Can you make it fly farther? How could you make a glider that flies in a circle?

Change your prototype and test it again, comparing the results with your first results. Have your improvements worked?

8: Communicate the design: Write up your project. Include diagrams and instructions so that someone else could make the same model or perhaps improve upon your design.

Real gliders are often launched by being towed behind powered planes.

GETTING INTO SPACE

Astronautical engineering is the branch of aerospace engineering that works with spacecraft. Drag and weight are different or non-existent in space, so the rules of aircraft design do not apply.

Lift off: The first challenge for any spacecraft is to escape Earth's gravity to get into space. Unlike most aircraft, rockets go straight up. The blast from the rocket comes out of the bottom and pushes the rocket vertically upward. The streamlined shape helps it cut through the air with minimum drag.

It takes a huge amount of thrust to force a rocket upward high enough to escape the atmosphere and Earth's field of gravity. Because of the large amount of fuel needed to achieve this, rockets are launched in stages—at least two and up to five. Each stage adds its own burst of thrust. After each stage, the part that held the fuel and engine is dropped. This reduces the weight of the remaining rocket and makes it easier for it to achieve the speed it needs. It also means that the engine for each stage can be suited to the conditions in which it will be used, such as lower temperatures.

JULIE PAYETTE—ENGINEER AND ASTRONAUT

Julie Payette was born in Montréal, Canada, in 1963. She trained as an engineer, and worked on advanced robotics systems used on the International Space Station. She was selected by the Canadian Space Agency in 1992 to train as an astronaut. Her training involved learning to fly military planes, deep-sea diving, and working in a reduced-gravity aircraft. On her mission on the Endeavour space shuttle, Payette operated the robotic arm, which helped a space-walking astronaut to install a laboratory on the outside of the space station. The laboratory was designed to allow experiments to be carried out in the **vacuum** of space.

Flying in space

In space, there is little gravity and no drag from the air. A streamlined shape is no longer necessary. With weight and drag greatly reduced, lift and thrust are easily obtained, so the spacecraft can speed through space using little fuel. As the distances covered in space are very great, this is important.

With such little thrust needed to move a spaceship through a vacuum, some future craft are being designed with sails. **Light radiation** from the sun will fall on the sails and provide enough force to drive the craft along.

Another possible way of changing the speed or direction of a spacecraft without using fuel is called gravity assist. The spacecraft can be treated a bit like a stone in a slingshot, whirled around the planet and thrown out into space.

Lightweight carbon fiber could be used to make a sail for a spacecraft.

LEARNING MORE

BOOKS

Hardesty, Von, *Flight*, Simon and Schuster, 2011

Mercer, Bobby, *The Flying Machine Book: Build and Launch 35 Rockets, Gliders, Helicopters, Boomerangs, and More*, Chicago Review Press, 2012

Nahum, Andrew, *Flight*, Dorling Kindersley, 2011

Skurzynski, Gloria, *This Is Rocket Science: True Stories of the Risk-taking Scientists who Figure Out Ways to Explore Beyond Earth*, National Geographic Children's Books, 2010

Solway, Andrew, *Aircraft*, Heinemann-Raintree, 2011

ONLINE

www.nasa.gov/audience/foreducators/nasaeclips/
A collection of short video clips from NASA providing clear explanations of many topics relating to aerospace engineering and flight and space travel.

http://airandspace.si.edu/education/onlinelearning.cfm
Online activities from the Smithsonian National Air and Space Museum to help you learn about flight and aviation history.

PLACES TO VISIT

Aero Space Museum of Calgary, Canada:
www.asmac.ab.ca

NASA Space Center, Houston, U.S.A:
www.spacecenter.org

The Smithsonian National Air and Space Museum, Washington, D.C., U.S.A:
http://airandspace.si.edu

GLOSSARY

aerodynamic Designed to reduce wind drag

aileron A hinged flap attached to the trailing edge of a wing, used to control the roll of an aircraft

airfoil A curved structure designed to provide lift and fight drag in flight

altitude The height above the ground or sea level

compressing Squashing or flattening by pressure

density The mass of a substance per unit of volume

elevator A hinged flap at the rear of an aircraft (often on a tail fin), used to control the pitch of an aircraft

gravity A force acting to pull objects with mass toward Earth

light radiation Energy emitted in the form of light

mass The measure of an object's resistance to gravity

molecule The smallest component of a material

pioneer A person who develops new ideas or techniques

propulsion The action of pushing forward

prototype A first model of a design built for testing

radar A system which uses radio waves to detect the presence of aircraft

regulations The rules made by an authority

rotor The rotating blades that provide lift for a helicopter

rudder A device used to steer a plane

symmetrical Made up of identical parts facing each other

vacuum A space in which there is no air

venturi tube A short piece of narrow tube between wider sections, used to measure the flow of a fluid

wind tunnel A tunnel where a stream of air is produced to test the effects of wind on models and full-size objects

INDEX